From Sagging to Success:
The Story of Emery Franklin

Florence M. Howard

Copyright © 2012, 2015 by Florence M. Howard
All rights reserved.

SSCOMM Publishing is a division of SSCOMM, Inc.
P.O. Box 753897, Memphis, Tennessee 38175-3897
www.sscommpr.com | info@sscommpr.com

Prints of artwork by Emery Franklin are available at
http://emery-franklin.artistwebsites.com

Library of Congress Control Number: 2012932249

ISBN-13: 978-0-6155-9772-0
ISBN-10: 0-6155-9772-6

FROM SAGGING TO SUCCESS
The Story of Emery Franklin

Illustrated by Emery Franklin
Cover Design and Book Layout by Frederick Virgous

DEDICATION

This book is dedicated to the 2011 Graduating Class of Booker T. Washington High School in Memphis, Tennessee, winner of President Barack Obama's Commencement Contest, and also to Zakkiyya Franklin who suggested her father's Crossroads: From Sagging to Success series of oil paintings would make a great book.

CONTENTS

	Acknowledgments	i
	Introduction	9
1	From Slavery to Sharecropping	14
2	Conscious Awakening	18
3	Civil Rights Era	22
4	1968	26
5	Focal Point	30
6	The Secret Found	34
7	Education is Key	38
8	The Beginning	42
9	Law of Attraction	46
10	Changing for the Better	50
11	The Black Woman	54
12	Think and Grow Rich	58
13	Secret of the Universe	62
14	Success	66
	Afterword	71
	Reading List	78

ACKNOWLEDGMENTS

The author and illustrator wish to thank the following individuals for sharing their thoughts and assisting with the development of this book: Tennessee State Representative Larry J. Miller, Cathy Ross, Robbie Franklin, Robert Robinson and Shasta Gavin.

INTRODUCTION

*Lives of great men all remind us
We can make our lives sublime,
And departing, leave behind us
Footprints on the sands of time.*

~ Henry Wadsworth Longfellow, *A Psalm of Life*

The world is filled with people who have special talents or gifts. They feel they can be great. They might not know yet how to apply their gift or how to improve it. In some cases, they actually don't know what their talent really is. But in their hearts and minds, they know they can and will be *GREAT*. The person may have an impairment or suffered an adversity that affects their self-esteem. Emery Franklin was that person.

Based on recent history, much is made of the fact that the latest wave of sagging came out of prison where inmates are denied belts for their loose-fitting uniforms. Most young people are unaware that prisoners were denied belts and forced to wear loose-fitting uniforms in order to differentiate them, prevent escape and humiliate them. Some inmates were taken advantage of by other inmates because of this practice. Moving back into the general population, this comfortable style made it onto the streets and then onto today's rap and hip-hop stage.

Sagging is the fashion style of intentionally wearing your pants so that your underwear shows. This style is much older than the last 15-20 years. The trend can be traced back to urban teenagers of the 1970's and the popularity of silk underwear. As one friend put it, "We sagged because it was cool and to show our manhood. It was our way of saying, 'Look! I'm wearing silk, these ain't cotton.'" If you're under the age of 15, ask your mother, grandmother, or aunt, if she wore bell-bottoms, platform shoes, halter tops and mini-skirts during her teens. Chances are she did. Fashion trends come and go, and come again.

MTV, BET, YouTube, and DVDs have transformed this 1970s rite of passage into a universal statement of individuality. It has lasted and lasted and crossed generational lines. Baby boomers in their 50's and 60's have been sagging along with their grandchildren.

The silk underwear fad had passed by the time Emery hit his teen years. Nevertheless, he lived in public housing and he felt the stigma. So, he always wanted to make a good impression. His attire was conscientious and neat. He didn't sag in the way he dressed ... but in his vision of himself.

One of six children, Emery Franklin grew up in a public housing development near Booker T. Washington High School. This was the first high school in Memphis built for blacks. Emery dreamed of being an artist. He didn't recognize his own gift until he was 12 or 13. His latent talent was encouraged by his mother, Ledora Franklin, and affirmed and nourished at Vance Junior High by his art teachers.

A graduate of BTW, Emery worked minimum wage jobs where he swept floors and performed other menial tasks. All the while, he dreamed of becoming a full-time artist. Yet, in the back of his mind remained a solitary thought. "I'm in the projects and I'm never going to get out of here."

But art and his God-given talent changed Emery Franklin's destiny and provided a way out. The week after he graduated, he became his own marketer. He painted, published and sold his work. By taking charge of his life, Emery changed his life. He viewed his talent as a gift from God, and felt in his heart that it was not God's plan for him to be a "starving artist." The question was: How to become a successful full-time artist? What is the secret to success?

He learned different painting techniques by studying the works of great artists. And, he diligently searched for the secret. His search led him to study the lives and the reflections of successful people. He read books on how to achieve success and greatness. In short, he educated himself.

Crossroads: From Sagging to Success

On display for an entire month, Emery's "Crossroads: From Sagging to Success" exhibition of 15 oil paintings opened at the Benjamin L. Hooks Central Library in Memphis on February 1, 2011. A box collected ties for Westside Middle School's two anti-sagging programs – Ties for Tuesday and The Urkel Initiative. Friends, family, former classmates and art lovers stopped by to view the exhibit. It was one of the library's most successful showings. On April 15, 2011, another of Emery's dreams came true when the exhibit was displayed outside the Thomas Kinkade Inspiration Art Gallery at Wolfchase Galleria. There, Emery greeted his eager fans and talked about the meaning of his work.

Emery's works are a positive expression of African American culture. As you study the pictures and read details about each one, you'll also hear from Emery himself. His intention is not to defend or denounce the fashion trend of sagging but to educate young people about their history and remind them that they are much more than the clothes on their backs. The painting series is not about the way you wear your clothes, that is a personal choice, it is about how you look at things, the way you think. Your thinking influences your actions and your actions determine your fate and your destiny. This book is subtitled *The Story of Emery Franklin* because it illustrates the path to success that Emery has taken.

In *From Sagging to Success*, the story is told through the eyes of a young man who is inspired to take a look at sagging, and its place in urban society. His name is Derrick and he contemplates the struggle for freedom and equality through the eyes of his ancestors. Like Emery, Derrick is searching for the secret to success. Once he finds it, he shares it with his family and friends.

As the series opens, Derrick is thinking about the history of African Americans and how Africans came to America's shores. He daydreams of a time after the 13th Amendment. In his mind, he envisions a man of African descent returning to his homeland, and his roots, on the continent of Africa.

13th Amendment to the U.S. Constitution: Abolition of Slavery

The House Joint Resolution proposing the 13th amendment to the Constitution, January 31, 1865; Enrolled Acts and Resolutions of Congress, 1789-1999; General Records of the United States Government; Record Group 11. Source: National Archives.

Paintings by Emery Franklin
"From Sagging to Success"

Chapter	Title	Page No.
1	*The Black Man*	15
2	*From Sun Up to Sun Down*	19
3	*Power of the Ballot*	23
4	*I AM A Man*	27
5	*Sagging*	31
6	*The Power of Positive Thinking*	35
7	*Education is Key*	39
8	*The Law of Success*	43
9	*Law of Attraction I (Rich Dad, Poor Dad)*	47
10	*Law of Attraction II*	51
11	*Law of Attraction III (Life is Good)*	55
12	*Think and Grow Rich*	59
13	*Secret of the Universe (My Book)*	63
14	*Success (Love)*	67
15	*My Man, The First Black President*	69

CHAPTER ONE

FROM SLAVERY TO SHARECROPPING

As long as the mind is enslaved, the body can never be free. Psychological freedom, a firm sense of self-esteem is the most powerful weapon against the long night of physical slavery.

~ Dr. Martin Luther King, Jr., civil and human rights activist

The first painting in the Crossroads exhibition is entitled *The Black Man*.

Derrick sees an ex-slave lying on a golden sand beach on the Gold Coast of Africa. The chain that once bound him and his ancestors for 400 years in America, *the long night of physical slavery*, was broken by the 13th Amendment to the U.S. Constitution that abolished slavery in 1865.

Interestingly, the man's body is free but the way he thinks about himself has not yet changed. He struggles with his innate knowledge of being a king in Africa and the former inferior and lowly treatment of him and his people in the Land of the Free and Home of the Brave.

It is almost moonset and the weary man lies with his strong arm outstretched toward the African village. He is an ex-slave who refused to remain enslaved and who left America because he was tired and weary of the sagging mindset that seems to be everywhere he went after he gained his freedom. Industrious and determined, he traveled in the boat he built himself.

The broken chain illustrates that he is free but not totally. There is conflict between how others see him and how he sees himself.

EMERY'S POINT

Emery painted *The Black Man* in 2009. There are nine links in the man's chain – possibly signifying the number of generations spent in slavery.

A visit to the Charles H. Wright Museum of African American History in Detroit gives visitors a personal and up close understanding of those generations spent in slavery. Traversing through the museum's 22,000 sq. ft. interactive exhibit – "And Still We Rise: Our Journey through African American History and Culture," museum patrons begin their journey in Africa. They witness the rise and fall of ancient and early modern civilizations. They cross the Atlantic and experience the tragedy of the Middle Passage. They come face to face with those who resisted bondage and emancipated themselves through avenues such as the Underground Railroad. The daunting experi-ence of standing in the life-size model of the belly of a slave ship gives new meaning to the phrase – only the strong survive.

There is a recurring debate about whether Abraham Lincoln signed the Emancipation Proclamation freeing those who were slaves in America for humanitarian or for political reasons. Such considerations cheapen the contributions of those who fought for that freedom. The fight against slavery was fought on many fronts and by many people, especially blacks who actively participated in the fight. The evidence is clear.

In *Free at Last: A Documentary History of Slavery, Freedom and the Civil War* which contains letters, personal testimony, official transcripts and records, the editors noted:

> With great immediacy, the letters depict the drama of emancipation in the midst of the nation's bloodiest conflict, and convey the struggle of black men and women to overthrow the slavery system, to aid the Union cause as laborers and soldiers and to give meaning to their newly won freedom in a war-torn nation. The documents show the active role of slaves and former slaves in transforming a war for the Union into a war against slavery, demonstrating, according to the *Journal of American History*, "that the destruction of slavery was accomplished through black self-determination."

Slave was a job description. Yet, some have internalized it as a stain upon their DNA. Viewing the condition of ancestral slavery as a spiritual and mental failing rather than a job description leads to unnecessary thoughts of inferiority. The cure is knowledge of African American history.

Emery wants you to ask yourself a question: Is there a link between the stain of slavery and sagging?

CHAPTER TWO
CONSCIOUS AWAKENING

Those who cannot remember the past are condemned to repeat it.

~ George Santayana, philosopher and novelist

The youth, Derrick remembers from American History that slavery was mostly in Southern states where cotton was "king." Slavery allowed America to become a great nation because slave labor was free labor. Cotton and free labor drove the economy and fueled the way of life in the South before and after the Civil War. In his mind, Derrick sees the cotton fields of the 1940's and thinks of his great-grandparents and grandparents who picked cotton in the nearby state of Mississippi.

Looking at the cotton field and then looking in the mirror, Derrick sees his own ill-fitting, sagging pants and oversized shirt. He admits to himself that he kind of dresses like a slave. He thinks of his parents and their nothing-can-change way of thinking. The sharecroppers toiling in the field cause him to wonder whether he and his parents are slaves to their way of thinking.

Is there such a thing as mental enslavement? He asks himself.

Is it possible that 150 years after the Emancipation Proclamation, he and others like him are still thinking of themselves as inferior? Is wearing saggy, ill-fitting clothes and celebrating ignorance by quitting school, being in debt,

not saving money, living above your income, and having children but not caring for them – just evidence of low self-esteem brought on by 550 years of outward and inward psychological torment?

Would being treated as a slave, stupid and worthless (except for your ability to cook, to clean, to work from sun up to sundown and to breed) mess with your mind? Was all that enough to influence generations after the Emancipation Proclamation to still see themselves as incapable of success?

Angrily, Derrick shakes his head in disbelief. Despite the what-ifs racing though his mind, he dares to seize the life-affirming thought: I want to be successful.

He thinks to himself. *I don't want to be a mental slave. This is America! I can do and be anything that I want in this country. Every day thousands and thousands of people in this country are making their dreams come true. Somewhere, somebody today is living the life that they dream of. I want to be somebody.*

He chooses his destiny: I can and will make my dreams come true.

EMERY'S POINT

The youth, standing and looking into the past, is sagging. Along with his sagging pants, he has a sagging mindset. At his feet is an open book signifying that he is in the midst of educating himself about African American history. In his mind, he sees his ancestors working from sunrise to sundown in the cotton fields. The boy is conscious that he has been asleep – unaware of the history of his people and his own family.

The dark sky symbolizes how back-breaking the work was and for very little reward. The pay was less than 25 cents an hour. Although better than not being paid at all, it was still what some called "slave wages." The life lived by African Americans in those days included the worst clothes, the worst food, the worst housing, and the worst opportunities for success.

Even so, Emery says "That happened. What are we going to do now?"

"What is the solution to how the young boys and girls think? How do we motivate them to exercise their intelligence and strive honorably for a better life?"

CHAPTER THREE
CIVIL RIGHTS ERA

Don't always be the victim. Because if you're the victim, you always lose.

~ Emery Franklin, fine artist

Reading books on African American history, Derrick realizes that the Civil Rights Movement was more than the few men and women his schools highlighted during a single month of the year. The Civil Rights Movement is the story of many people making a decision to make a difference. Martin Luther King, Jr. was one of thousands who fought for freedom and equality.

President Andrew Johnson in 1865 pardoned wealthy supporters of the Confederacy. In 1866, he expanded the power of the Freedmen's Bureau and ex-slaves made tremendous strides. During this Reconstruction Period, some blacks became sharecroppers while other African Americans excelled in business, education, medicine, science and government. However, the 1876 presidential election changed things: freedmen lives became more difficult due to the Jim Crow laws enacted between 1876 and 1965.

The U.S. Supreme Court in 1896 aided segregationists when, in *Plessy v. Ferguson*, it ruled that the use of "separate but equal" facilities was legal. This resulted in more second-class citizenship for blacks in the South. Blacks could not attend the same schools as whites. They were barred from enjoying public attractions like the circus or the fair on the same days as whites and from sitting together in concerts, movie theaters, ball games and restaurants. Blacks

could not try on clothes in white-owned stores. There were separate water fountains, restrooms, and seating on public transportation.

On May 17, 1954 in *Brown v. Board of Education of Topeka*, the U.S. Supreme Court ruled state laws establishing separate public schools for black and white students were unconstitutional. The *Brown* decision overturned *Plessy v. Ferguson*. A year and a half later, Rosa Parks decided not give up her bus seat in Montgomery, Alabama. Although she was not the first to refuse, her action led to the Montgomery Bus Boycott. The boycott ended December 20, 1956, when the Court declared Alabama and Montgomery laws requiring segregated buses unconstitutional. These unconstitutional laws also affected the ability of blacks to vote. Poll taxes, literacy tests and grandfather clauses kept blacks from voting in some states. Those who worked registering people to vote were jailed, beaten and even killed. The Civil Rights Act of 1964 outlawed discrimination against blacks and women, and the Voting Rights Act of 1965 outlawed discriminatory voting practices, including racial gerrymandering of political districts.

In his mind, Derrick sees the hand holding a voting ballot. He now understands what black people went through to vote. He is becoming more aware that he is blessed. He decides, he will be a voter.

EMERY'S POINT

The *Power of the Ballot* illustrates the commitment of African Americans in the 1960's. They and others fought to secure the voting rights of blacks and displayed the courage needed to exercise that right. The blood on the arm of the voter in the foreground represents the blood shed by Fannie Lou Hamer, Medgar Evers, James Chaney and countless courageous others who took a stand against discriminatory voting practices.

The history of nearly every successful African American during the last 150 years is a personal movement from "slavery" to sagging to success. To move forward from sagging to success, Emery believes we must change our mindset. Like the Civil Rights Movement, this change takes courage, determination and commitment.

Dr. Wayne Dyer said, "Change the way you look at things and the things you look at change." That's Emery all-time favorite quotation. Regarding the Civil Rights Movement, it means that you can look at the struggle for civil rights and equality as a series of battles fought and won (victor) or as an oppressive listing of insults and injury (victim). As one historian pointed out, only survivors survived the Middle Passage. You get to choose how you see black history and yourself. Changing your point of view from victim to victor influences your thoughts, beliefs and actions.

Emery also has spent a great deal of time reading about history and religion. "I need to know where I came from so that I know where I can go," he said.

The presidential race of Barack Obama in 2008 gave young people a positive reason to vote. Millions were inspired by his "Yes We Can" slogan.

Voting today is just as important as it was in 2008 and 2012. History records that it was once against the law for blacks and women to vote. The 15th and 19th Amendments changed things. The Voting Rights Act of 1965 made those amendments real by outlawing race-based discriminatory practices and putting the ballot into the hands of black men and black women who registered to vote without the albatross of legalized discrimination.

Voting means we understand the importance of the sacrifices made by those who shed blood to obtain recognition of full citizenship. Accordingly, our votes honor the people who fought for civil rights and equality. Just as importantly, voting means that we realize the significance and impact of the U.S. political system in our daily lives from the cradle to the grave. On the local, state and federal levels, elected officials control how tax dollars and resources are divided and distributed, and what laws are passed in support of or in opposition to individual and group interests.

CHAPTER FOUR
1968

Whether you have a Ph.D., or no D, we're in this bag together. And whether you're from Morehouse or Nohouse, we're still in this bag together.

~ Fannie Lou Hamer, Mississippi voting rights activist

The I AM A MAN sign is something that Derrick had seen commemorated every year of his life. Although he was not born until well after the 1968 Memphis Sanitation Workers Strike -- its significance is inescapable for Memphis residents. He knew the basics. Dr. Martin Luther King, Jr., a Morehouse College graduate, came to town to help striking garbage workers.

Black employees in the Memphis Public Works Department endured racial discrimination for many years. They had asked for better treatment, better pay and safer working conditions but nothing changed. On February 1, a rainy day, something horrible happened: Sanitation workers Echol Cole and Robert Walker were killed in a work-related accident. It seemed that the men had died in vain since there was no mention of them in the newspaper or on the TV news. Galvanized by such disregard, 1300 black sanitation workers walked off the job in protest 10 days later.

The famed *I've Been to the Mountaintop* speech was made on April 3, 1968 at Mason Temple Church of God in Christ. Dr. King was assassinated the following day at the Lorraine Motel, now the site of the renowned National Civil Rights Museum.

Jesse Epps, the man who coined the legendary "I am a Man" phrase used on the signs of striking workers was one of the men Dr. King came to help. In fact, he was on the balcony when Dr. King was slain. The strike lasted until April 16, 1968 when officials of the AFSCME Labor Union 1733 announced a settlement had been reached. The workers gained union recognition and wage increases. In 2011, Mr. Epps and the entire group of workers were inducted into the U.S. Department of Labor Hall of Fame.

This history made Derrick hungry for more. He decided to visit the museum to see what else he could learn about the strike, Dr. King and the Civil Rights Movement.

EMERY'S POINT

Among the paintings in progress in Emery's studio is a single computer-generated sign. Taped on his studio wall, the sign reads: "Change the way you look at things and the things you look at change." This quote from Dr. Wayne Dyer, an internationally-known, best-selling author and motivational speaker, provides Emery with focus, inspiration and motivation.

"The Black Man" returned to Africa. He went through a lot but was strong enough to break the chains of mental slavery. "We can't go back to Africa," said Emery, "but we can break that mental slavery by changing the way we think. It is a proven fact, people who think positively of themselves accomplish more than those who are think negatively of themselves."

The first four paintings in the Crossroads series covered phases of Black history. Viewing slavery as 400 years of free labor, Emery said, "If you look at how America and the world have advanced, you'll see that America, England, France, and the Caribbean came up fast, and we did a lot for the world because we did it free."

"We are not poor because we didn't want to work but because we did not profit from our work," said Emery. "I believe in reparations. We should be getting paid back for all our free work, hard sweat and mental stress. We can change the way we think and get rich, too, by doing business globally."

Dr. Dyer in his book, *The Power of Intention*, posted this quote from Buckminster Fuller: "Everyone is born a genius, but the process of living de-geniuses them." The process of slavery, living as second-class citizens and being denied civil and human rights certainly had a lingering effect on the genius of African Americans. Even so, now is the time to move forward.

In his ten-step program on activating your genius, Dr. Dyer stated that Step 1 is declaring yourself to be a genius. "This shouldn't be a public pronouncement," he wrote, "but a statement of intention between you and your Creator."

Emery has declared himself to be a genius who proudly recognizes the genius in others.

CHAPTER FIVE
FOCAL POINT

African-Americans define and redefine what's stylish and cool....For some adolescents this style might actually increases their self-esteem ....
For another person this type of dress could lead to antisocial behavior.

~ Dr. Wendy Buskey, clinical psychologist

The fashion police have arrived. According to various magazine articles and online reports, between 2005 and 2008 at least five cities and towns – Delcambre, La., Opelousas, Ill., Lynwood, Ill., Riviera Beach, Fla., and Flint, Mich. – passed ordinances making sagging pants a crime punishable with warnings, fines, community service and possible jail time for habitual offenders. Fines ranged from $25 in Lynwood to $150 in Riviera Beach to $500 and 6 months in jail in Delcambre. Arrests were made in Flint. Meanwhile, the American Civil Liberties Union has argued sagging pants is a constitutional right. In 2011, Tennessee state legislators refused a public sagging law. However, a later bill requiring public schools to address the issue of exposed underwear and body parts, in the student handbook, passed with overwhelming support. The law took effect July 1, 2012.

Derrick slowly came out of his historical daydream. Reflecting on his life, he wondered at the choices he had made. In his world, success was defined by music video moguls who sang about making it to the top of the charts or having lots of girl friends. Freedom was bling, hip-hop designer clothes with matching Nikes, baggy pants, big shirts and lots of girls. Freedom was the car you drove and having enough money to make it rain in the club on a

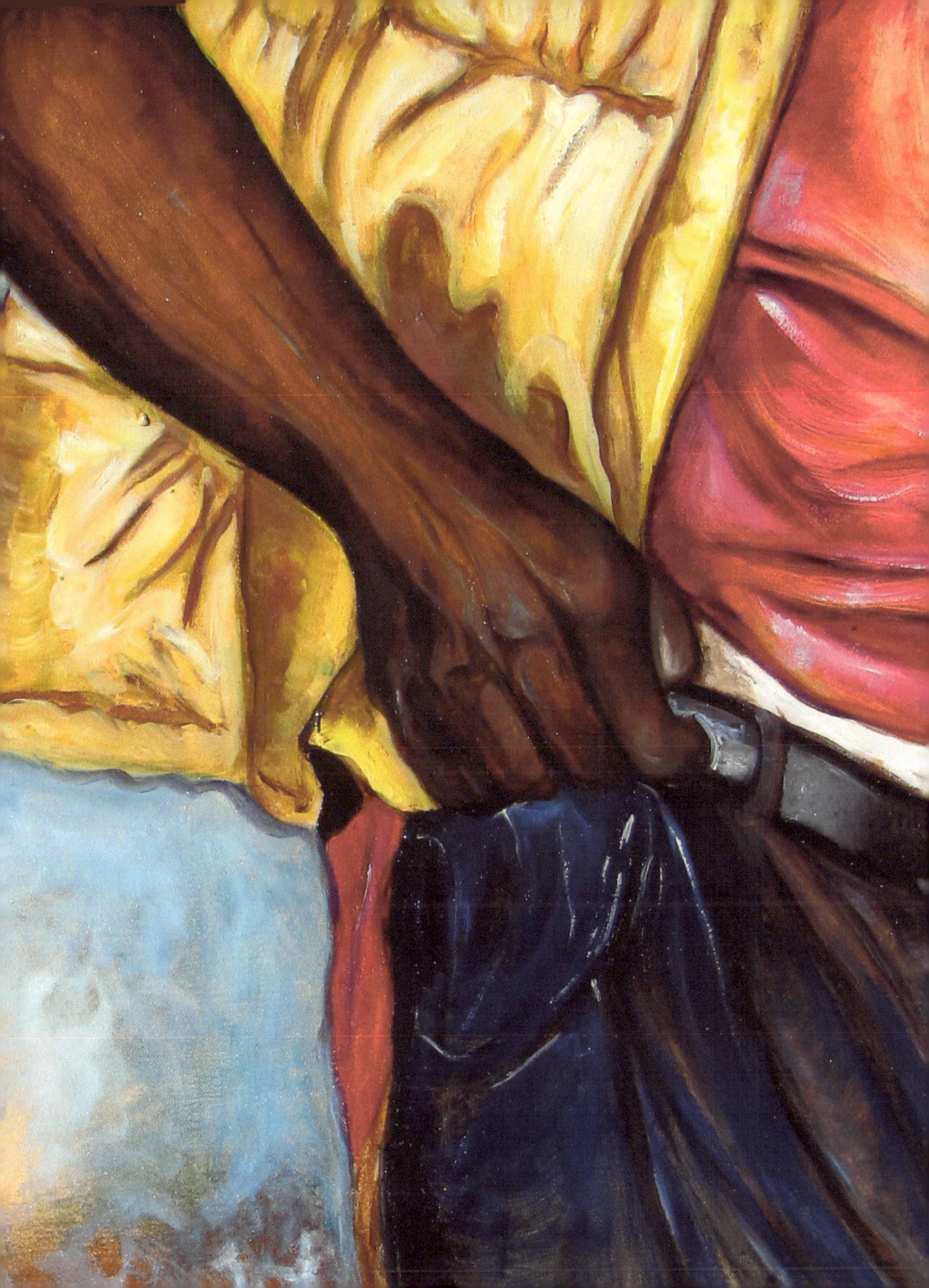

Friday night. Sagging was about being stylish and cool not about committing a crime. If sagging is criminalized, there will be more young blacks and their white counterparts with criminal records.

Derrick's mind went back to the pictures and words in the history books – slaves in baggy clothes, special laws against black people, and the struggle for dignity. Catching a glimpse of himself in the mirror, he saw his red Rocawear tee shirt reached his thighs and Sean John jean shorts went past the knees. Beneath the shirt was 3 to 4 inches of white TH underpants. He thought about those who said sagging came right out of prison, where belts aren't allowed. As he viewed his mirrored image, his hand all on its own reached down to his belt and pulled the pants up.

EMERY'S POINT

Painting No. 5, *Sagging* is the focal point of the exhibit. The boy's new way of thinking about himself is influencing his actions. That hand is on the pants, pulling them up.

Emery said that we should try to remember everything that we've been through.

Way back when, people lived in raggedy shacks. They used ropes to hold their pants up. They put paper in the bottom of their shoes when the soles wore out. People didn't buy new clothes, they made them and wore them as long as they could. If they were in a big family, they passed the clothes down to younger brothers and sisters. If the clothes were really old and raggedy, their grandmother ripped them up and put the pieces into quilts to help keep them warm in the winter. We have come a long way individually and as a group.

When you think differently, you act differently. Raised in a Brooklyn, N.Y. housing project and abandoned by his father, Jay-Z is a high school drop-out who used to sell drugs. Now, he is married and a father. His real name is Shawn Carter. He is a rapper, actor, record producer, and entrepreneur with a net worth of over $450 million in 2010. He has sold more than 50 million albums and has won 13 Grammy Awards. Creator of the Rocawear line, he has investments in a night club, a NBA basketball team and much more. He has gone from sagging to success.

You've come a long way, baby.

CHAPTER SIX
THE SECRET FOUND

I discovered The Secret, and everything in my life -- including my company – was totally transformed, because I changed the way I was thinking.

~ Jack Canfield, best-selling author and success coach

Derrick continued reading all kinds of books. From American and African American history books, he learned about the dignity of men and women like Frederick Douglas and Sojourner Truth who fought to be free from slavery in the 1860's. He learned about W.E.B. DuBois and George Washington Carver who worked to improve life in the 1940's. Other books, stories and storytelling witnesses introduced him to Diane Nash, Rev. James Lawson, and Rev. Henry Logan Starks who stood up for civil and human rights in Tennessee during the 1960's.

From there, he turned his attention to books about business and books by and about successful people. He became an eager reader in his search for the truth and the secret. He had heard TV preachers say that God is no respecter of persons. In that case, whatever the rich knew and he didn't, he could find out.

"Education is definitely the key," Derrick said, after reading a few of the books successful people read and recommended. "If I read the books that they read, I can actually do the same thing that they have done" was his ever-present thought.

He decided Bob Johnson, the founder of BET, and Don Thompson, who took over as president of McDonald's USA in 2006 and then became CEO of McDonald's Corp. in 2012, must have read the books he was reading.

Derrick was sagging his pants some of the time. He was reading all of the time.

EMERY'S POINT

From Tupac to Will Smith to Lil Wayne, sagging is a way of bobbing to the music of life. It's a phase -- and you need to keep the big picture in mind. There is a process that you go through to be successful. Rappers work hard at reading and writing, and they learn the business side of their business. The majority don't have a formula for success. But watch Russell Simmons or P. Diddy (Sean Combs), and you'll see the Law of Attraction in operation. Up and coming music mogul, Mickey Wright Jr. used the Law of Attraction to visualize his future in the music industry (*Conversation Piece*, Jan/Feb. 2008). He went from sweeping floors at the record company to being known worldwide as "Memphis Hitz." Some folks call him "Young Diddy."

At 6 ft. 1 in., Emery was a standout at Booker T. Washington where he played guard and offensive tackle on the football team. During his junior year, Valley State University, Georgia Tech and Austin Peay offered him scholarships. "I had done my research and I knew that 99% of those guys [college football players] don't go pro," he said. "I would have played for four years and made some people a lot of money. I knew that I had to get a real education because chances of going pro were slim."

Emery, then a senior, hurt his knee in game five of 1980. After graduation, he enrolled in Memphis Academy of Art. There, he discovered his artistic techniques had advanced beyond those taught in first year classes. The instructors used his work as example for other students. To learn more himself, he sat in on more advanced classes. He quit after his first year. Student loans were not part of his success plan. He decided to rely on his artistic talent and continue teaching himself new skills.

Reading *Rich Dad, Poor Dad* in 1995, Emery Franklin was inspired to be more conscious about finances and business. "When you have an opportunity to be successful, you need to take it," he said. He kept his eyes open for opportunities and got a job cleaning planes at Northwest Airlines. He and co-worker Michael Brown began using their travel privileges for weekly trips to L.A. -- buying handbags, rings, watches, silk ties, suits, and shoes directly from manufacturers for resell in Memphis. Some things he bought for $10 could be sold for $75-$100. Later, Emery and his wife traveled to Hawaii to buy pearls and made them into earrings to sell.

Emery painted at night and used the money he made to invest in real estate. More importantly, he kept on reading. *Rich Dad, Poor Dad* was followed by two Napoleon Hill books, *Law of Success* and *Think and Grow Rich*.

CHAPTER SEVEN
EDUCATION IS KEY

The function of education is to teach one to think intensively and to think critically. Intelligence plus character - that is the goal of true education.

~ Dr. Martin Luther King, Jr., preacher, activist, author

Observe Derrick, the young man in Emery's painting. He has continued reading and putting into practice what he learns. He too has read *Rich Dad, Poor Dad* and other books that successful people read so his way of thinking is changing more and more. He has stopped watching negative videos and reading negative books.

Ever thirsty to know the secret of success, he was watching *The Oprah Winfrey Show* when millionaire TV icon Oprah introduced Rhonda Byrne, creator of the "The Secret" movie. The viewers who tuned into Oprah that day in 2006 heard Byrne give the secret away. By following the philosophy explained in the movie, she said anyone could have the successful life, the money, the health, the job and the relationships they desired. Derrick bought the DVD and watched it over and over again. He began to think positively about life and stopped thinking someone was always trying to take something away from him. He realized that he has something valuable to give.

The Secret is the Law of Attraction: Whatever you think about consistently good or bad comes to you. You attract what you think about.

Derrick, wearing the cap and green vest, is reading another of his new books. Newly educated about the powerful Law of Attraction, he is thinking positively. He is not like the guy in the orange vest that has no head. That guy is not thinking at all.

Thoughts influence action and actions influence your destiny.

EMERY'S POINT

Once the boy read the first book, he was hungry to know more. Learning more about the power of positive thinking, he began to see a root problem -- a strange form of hopelessness caused by negative thinking. Ironically, he had been working against himself. Double-mindedness had been canceling out his best efforts and delaying his success.

Emery said, "Once you want something, you've got to believe you're going to get it. Follow the formula. Thinking we can't do it or that someone has their foot on our back is a problem."

As the old adage says, when you know better you do better.

There is a school building is in the painting because in Emery's opinion "if you want to know something, school is where you start. That's why you need to go to school."

Without education, formal or informal training, parent- or teacher-aided learning or self-study, it is nearly impossible to be successful. When a baby learns to walk, pediatricians say, the process is driven by emotional, social and physical interaction. The child sees her parent walking and desires to walk as well. She does the physical labor; and, the emotional and social encouragement she gets is part of the process. The personal desire to learn, to know and to understand is paramount and lack of this inward drive is the reason many people choose failure rather than success. You must be hungry: You must want to know. You must desire to succeed. Moreover, unlike a baby who is gets lots of outside encouragement, you will most likely need to encourage yourself. Believe in yourself even when no one else does.

Seek to understand and to think for yourself because education is the key. To think is to process information you see, hear and read. Learning is acquiring new or improved awareness (knowledge), skills, behaviors, values and preferences. This is an ability that humans share with animals and with machines like computers, robots and your smartphone.

Thinking positively leads you away from negative thinking and from negative people. The books on the ground in the painting are some of Emery's favorites because they influenced him the most. Through reading them, he gained new awareness, skills, behaviors and preferences that enable him to make better choices.

CHAPTER EIGHT
THE BEGINNING

"The mind of the prudent acquires knowledge, and the ear of the wise seeks knowledge."

~ Proverbs 18:15 (New American Standard Bible)

Knowledge is said to be the beginning of wisdom.

Derrick is acquiring more knowledge, reading more books on success – the same books that rich people read. He is becoming successful. He is starting to do business and make money.

His knowledge and appreciation for the world and other cultures grow. He realizes how much ancient Egypt and Africa contributed to the world in mathematics, science, medicine, literature, architecture, art and technology.

EMERY'S POINT

Many people don't realize that there is a formula, a Law of Success. If you use the law, you become successful. In *The Law of Success* painting, modern-day men and women stroll through ancient Egypt. Books flow from the foundation of the pyramids in Giza to show Egypt, located on the continent of Africa, as a source of America's greatness. The first blacks who came to America were not slaves. They were skilled mariners, craftsmen and artisans.

Emery has his own viewpoint. "From Africa to today, something went wrong. They [slave traders] didn't go to get dumb people but the smartest they could find. Black people aren't dumb – we've done a lot for the world. Black people invented the stoplight, the cell phone and a whole lot more. Kids should be reaping the benefits of the work of their parents and fore-parents. But that is not happening. The world owes us something but not in the way we think."

Every book that Emery reads goes into his home library. His favorites are *Rich Dad, Poor Dad, Science of Success, The Power of Intention, Think and Grow Rich, Power vs. Force, Your Invisible Power*, and *The Power of Vision*. While books titled in the painting have influenced his thinking the most, he also uses DVDs like "The Secret" and watches YouTube interviews about successful people and those offering fresh ideas on success, marketing and networking. Learning for Emery is a lifelong enterprise.

He credits Memphis businessman Frank Banks with giving him his first big break as an artist when he commissioned him to illustrate the cover of the 1995 African American Historical Calendar. Using what he learned from reading and from Mr. Banks, Emery soon came up with a plan to sell 1000 copies of his artwork. He painted, printed and sold the prints at a massive public event that attracted 400,000 people. Within a couple of days, he had earned the $10,000 that he and his wife needed for a special family project. He has been with the same printer for years so preparing high quality photos and ordering his own prints wasn't a new thing. After all, he has been painting, publishing and selling his creations since high school. Selling a thousand prints in the space of a few days, however, was new. And, it showed him that the Law of Attraction works!

"I was reading like crazy," recalled Emery, "I'm reading like I have never read in my life. When I read *Power vs. Force*, it made me really see things differently."

In addition to reading, Emery meditates every day to attract the positive things that he wants in his life. By reading books and studying the work of other artists, he taught himself various painting techniques that he uses. He is a musician who taught himself to play the piano. He also designed the first album cover for Memphis-born record producer/rapper Drumma Boy (aka Christopher James Gholson). Almost daily, Emery's successes prove that knowledge, knowing what you want, believing you shall have it, and a positive attitude open doors.

Emery has a creative mind and, according to prosperity writer Wallace Wattles, we all do. In his *Science of Getting Rich*, Wattles wrote, "Man is a thinking center, capable of original thought; if man can communicate his thought, he can cause creation, or formation, of the thing he thinks about."

Creative African American Inventors

Plato called necessity, the mother of invention. Speaking of invention, a great debt is owed to Henry E. Baker, an assistant patent examiner in the U.S. Patent Office during the late 1800s and early 1900s. His 1913 book, *The Colored Inventor: A Record of Fifty Years*, listed more than 250 inventions patented by black people. You will find out more about the contributions of black inventors and innovators at the back of this book, beginning on page 75.

CHAPTER NINE
LAW OF ATTRACTION

There is nothing wrong in wanting to be rich. The desire for riches is really the desire for a richer, fuller and more abundant life.

~Wallace D. Wattles, author of *Science of Getting Rich*

Derrick's father is a farmer. The family lives in an old shack on land that has been in the family for decades. While they once saw themselves as dirt-poor, they now consider themselves land-rich. The transformation in thinking is because the father is reading the books that his son is reading. He realizes that if you have land, you have wealth.

Wealth has started to come to him because his thinking and how he sees himself have changed. He has become wise in handling his money and in planting crops to sell. For example, he used to go to the market and spend the money there.

Now, he brings the money home. His desire for a richer, fuller and more abundant life is coming true.

EMERY'S POINT

Emery uses the Law of Attraction successfully. He continually practices three simple steps.

First, he asks for what he wants. He says what he wants to happen, out loud, to his wife, to his friends and to people he meets. People might look at him curiously and may doubt that what he's said will happen, but he dismisses their doubts. He is confident. After all, he knows the Law of Attraction works. He has faith.

The sad truth is that many people are better able to say what they don't want quicker and more confidently than what they do want. This means they get more of what they don't want. That is how the law works. They are attracting what they think about and talk about most. All of us have talked about someone that we haven't heard from in a while and then run into that person on the street or get a phone call. That's the Law of Attraction at work. Some people want others to agree with them before they believe their idea themselves but not Emery. The fact that he believes it gives him the excitement to go forward.

Secondly, he visualizes doing or having the thing or experience that he wants. He gets excited about it. He envisions himself doing that very thing. For example, since he's an artist, he wants his art in lots of galleries, all over the country. In April 2011, his artwork was put into the Memphis Thomas Kinkade Inspiration Gallery for the first time.

Emery was the first African American artist to be displayed and sold in the gallery. It took three years but it finally happened. For three years, he'd stop by the gallery on a regular basis. Here's another example. Having his art at the Benjamin L. Hooks Central Library in Memphis was once just a dream. He told the curator that he wanted to exhibit there, she gave him the guidelines and he created the Crossroads series especially for the library. Now, he's had two exhibits there.

Lastly, he expects it to happen. For the first library exhibit, all of the pictures were lined up in his brain waiting to come out even before the library had accepted the idea. Emery, ever proactive, went to talk with them because he doesn't just sit and dream. He goes forward and makes contact with an expectation that what he wants will come true. The *Law of Success* painting with the Egyptian pyramids was the first in the series to pop out of his head and onto the canvas. When Emery has an idea, he doesn't sit on it. He moves into action. Because he envisions himself in lots of galleries, he calls 50 galleries each month throughout the U.S. to see if they are accepting new artists.

"I meditate a lot and thank God for everything. So, I plan out my whole day before my day starts. If you meditate, you get ideas that you wouldn't have ever thought of on your own. You expect those things to go exactly as you say that you want it to go because you are thankful," said Emery. "Be thankful and don't complain about anything."

Out of habit, you might occasionally doubt or think negatively. Rewind. Stop right there and remind yourself of everything you have to be thankful for (your parents, brothers, sisters, friends, teachers and mentors … sunshine, rain, this book) and all the great things that are coming your way.

Emery reminds you to stay positive and think big: "Some people say, 'I want to be able to pay my bills.' But God, I want to have no bills."

CHAPTER TEN
CHANGING FOR THE BETTER

I am changing, trying every way I can
I am changing, trying to be better than I am

~ "I am Changing" lyrics, *Dreamgirls* (1981)

The farmer has started to think differently. With the money from marketing his crops, he has purchased a tractor. The tractor is a wise use of his money because it allows him to plant more crops on his land.

Using the Law of Attraction, he is attracting more of what he wants in his life. Now instead of one bucket of money to take home, he has two buckets. Their whole family life is changing. He is still going home to a shack but his thinking has changed.

EMERY'S POINT

Emery's maternal grandfather was a farmer. Back in those days, you could buy an acre of land for less than $10. During the Great Depression of the 1930's, African Americans and poor whites in the Mississippi Delta existed on grounded grain, meat and molasses. It was difficult to get your product to market and difficult to sell it because there was little money available. Some farmers were paid by the government to take their land out of production in order to increase demand. Those who benefited from the program were generally wealthy planters who "employed" lots of sharecroppers, some as many as 100 or more. Without the need to raise a harvest for sale, many sharecroppers were turned out, evicted. This was especially true if the planter or landowner disapproved of you.

It was said that the remedy for sharecropping was to own land, something that Emery's grandfather did. He was a small landowner in Mississippi. However, in later years, the family lost or sold the land because they thought of it as a burden rather than a means to build wealth. "If you have land," said Emery, "you have wealth but they didn't understand."

When you think differently, you act differently. The farmer in the painting has changed his thinking. In the first of three pictures showing him in his field, he has one bucket of money. In the painting in this chapter, he has two money pots – a blue pail and a white bucket – as well as a new tractor. He purchased the tractor when he bought more land so that he could work 1000 acres instead of the 300 he already had. Learning more about land management, he planted warm season row crops -- tomatoes, okra, peppers, eggplant, potatoes, cucumbers, squash and melons in the spring and summer – and cool season crops like greens, turnips, spinach, beans, peas, onions, rutabagas, pumpkin and more squash in the fall. He used multiple planting techniques and rotated some crops every two to three years to replenish the nutrients in the soil. He has grown from a farmer into a businessman who sells his product not only at farmer's markets but also in restaurants and food stores.

He is attracting more and more of what he wants. If you know your vision, keep your mind on your purpose and do everything that you must do and can do, everyday, to the best of your ability, you will be successful.

Someone once said that successful people do what unsuccessful people are not willing to do. That means getting up early and working until the job is finished. The truly successful perform every job well and they keep their word. They also show genuine gratitude.

Unfortunately, there are those who have turned hard work and successful achievements like good grades, paying your bills on time and getting an education into something that others are supposed to be ashamed of.

The Law of Attraction is simply this: you reap what you sow. If you do the crime, you'll do the time. If you put in the time, you will shine.

CHAPTER ELEVEN

THE BLACK WOMAN, OUR BACKBONE AND INSPIRATION

I don't shout or jump about | Or have to talk real loud.
When you see me passing, | It ought to make you proud.

~ Maya Angelou, author, poet, historian

The farmer brings the money home to his wife. She is barefooted and sitting on a plastic bucket on the porch of the shack. She has been reading the books of the rich and successful too. She is the money-counter. She realizes that they have made a mistake in their old way of thinking. And, she's correcting that mistake and preparing to take the family to the next level, real fast. As she looks into the distance, she visualizes, meditates and celebrates the future.

EMERY'S POINT

In Emery's opinion, the main reason African Americans have succeeded is because of the Black Woman. "She has always been the backbone of the family to get us where we need to go. 'She can take 15 cents and turn it into a dollar.' In church, in business and raising her children, this woman excels. She is the virtuous woman whose children "arise up and call her blessed."

President Abraham Lincoln said that everything he was and ever hoped to be, he owed to his mother. The same can be said for every woman who puts the needs of her family before her own personal needs, wants and desires.

This is especially true of the black women who raise their children and those of others, in slavery and beyond, to make them into good and confident people. No matter her situation, the good mother does her best. That is the point of this painting. *The Black Woman*, sitting next to a pile of money, could have bought herself new shoes and new clothes while living in a shack. Instead of living for today, she claimed a rich future. She and her family would have it all, everything they wanted for body, mind, soul and spirit.

Who is the Black Woman?

She is the mother, grandmother, foster parent, sister, aunt or neighbor who motivates and encourages you to be your best. She sets high standards and tells you that you are smart and you can be anything or have anything you desire if you are willing to work hard to get it. She is the significant other who tells you that she believes you can be a successful rapper, businessman, doctor, lawyer or whatever you desire and that she stands behind you 100 percent.

She is the woman with the child who stutters, who is sick, who is disabled or who is emotionally scarred or intellectually challenged. Yet, she refuses to accept limiting labels that predict what the child cannot do or achieve. She is an amazing woman worthy of respect. She opens schools, colleges, churches, daycare centers and after-school programs because she sees a need. She runs soup kitchens to feed the hungry and the homeless. To help support her family, she goes into business – opening restaurants, cleaning services and daycare centers – or works two jobs. She donates her time freely to young people and still makes time to understand, motivate and encourage her own children.

The Black Woman has more than the proverbial diamonds in her backyard, she is a flawless diamond. Stories are told and repeated. Poems and songs have been written about her faithfulness, courage, strength, spirituality, intelligence, and wisdom.

CHANGE THE WAY YOU LOOK AT THE BLACK WOMAN, AND THE WAY YOU LOOK AT HER CHANGES.

CHAPTER TWELVE
THINK AND GROW RICH

Patience, persistence and perspiration make an unbeatable combination for success.

~Napoleon Hill, author, journalist, attorney

The farmer is still walking his field but the house is new. The family is reaping the benefits of their son finding the secret. You don't see the son but he is inside the house reading and thinking about business. He is the business manager of the family.

The Black Woman standing on the porch of the grand house is dressed in lovely clothes and shoes. She waves a welcoming hand to her husband. The field is green with row upon row of new crops, promising an abundant harvest to come. The man has money both in the pail and in his back pocket.

In countless ways in mind, body, soul and spirit -- the family has become wealthy due to their new way of thinking.

EMERY'S POINT

The woman found and bought the house, Emery said, and put it on the same spot where the shack once stood. The entire family – the son, the father and the mother are using the Law of Attraction.

Law of Attraction coach, Michael J. Losier wrote a book entitled *Law of Attraction: The Science of Attracting More of What You Want and Less of What You Don't.*

In his book, he gives techniques for using the Law of Attraction. Using worksheets, he helps adults figure out what they want, why they don't have it already, and what they need to do to get it.

There is a special section for parents and teachers who want to teach the techniques to children. Losier said, "Imagine having everyone in your family or classroom practicing the Law of Attraction." For children, he uses the word *vibes* instead of *vibrations* to describe how the way your thinking influences what you attract. Negative thinking has a negative vibe. Positive thinking has a positive vibe. He said that children can learn from their own experience in order to understand the effects of negative and positive thinking. He has young people write the words: Don't, Not and No, in big letters.

Those three words are used when someone feels negative. He said, too much of what children hear from adults is "don't be late," "don't get dirty," "don't run," "no bullying," and the like. Just saying those words out loud or hearing them make children feel negative. Losier's technique for turning on a positive vibe is to use a "secret." His secret involves switching on a positive vibe every time you hear yourself saying "don't," "not" or "no" by asking yourself, "So, what do I want?"

Michael Losier said that saying what you want makes you feel better than saying and focusing on what you don't want. The next time, a parent, brother, sister or friend uses the negative words, you should quietly ask the secret question – "So, what do you want?" Losier suggests wearing a wide rubber band or medallion and labeling it "Secret." The band becomes a reminder to ask the question, "So, what do I want?"

In his family, Emery is the king of the Law of Attraction. His daughter, Zakkiyya, who also paints, uses positive vibes and his wife, Robbie, likewise. Each member of the family has permission to quietly point out when they notice one of the others using don't, not and no. It rarely happens but every once in a while, Emery gets a reminder. Emery talks about the Law of Attraction with practically everyone he meets – gallery owners, other artists, family members -- because he knows the Law of Attraction works for old and young.

"You may not be aware of it but a very powerful force is present in your life. It's called the Law of Attraction and right now it's attracting people, jobs, situations, and relationships to you," said Michael Losier as he encourages his readers. "Learn how to use it deliberately and make it work for you."

CHAPTER THIRTEEN
SECRET OF THE UNIVERSE

Children are made readers on the laps of their parents.

~ Emilie Buchwald, children's book author

The young child, Derrick's son, is the new or next generation. Comfortable and content, he sits on the floor in the house of his grandfather, the successful farmer. The library is filled with the child's own books and those of his grandfather, grandmother, father and mother. Because all of them took turns reading to him, he learned to love reading at an early age. Like all avid readers, he has discovered that he can go around the world in books and learn all kinds of knowledge and skills.

Reading helps him to imagine all the things he wants to be, the kind of life that he would like to have, and the places that he would love to go.

EMERY'S POINT

Emery strongly believes that reading is the key to a successful life.

When you read the books that successful people read, you learn to think the way they think. They think differently from the average person. Rich folks go around the world while those who are poorer sit and watch because they see the world totally different. Reading opens up doors that no one can close. Once you've learned something, no one can take it away from you. Reading has multiple benefits.

As every librarian and teacher knows,
1. Reading builds self-esteem. Your new knowledge gives you confidence and others admire your knowledge.

2. Reading gives you a look into other cultures, lifestyles, customs and places in the world.

3. Reading gives you something to talk about.

4. Reading improves your creativity by developing the creative part of your brain.

5. Reading improves your discipline by giving you an opportunity to finish something you start.

6. Reading improves your memory for details.

7. Reading improves your vocabulary. You become a better speller and a better writer.

8. Reading increases your concentration and ability to focus.

9. Reading keeps you from feeling bored.

10. Reading makes you smarter by training your brain to think. Those who read generally score higher on IQ tests.

Studies have shown that parents who read to their children even while they are in the womb help their child's brain to develop. Listening toddlers gain a better grasp of language and are better talkers. Because children learn to concentrate during story time, attention spans are longer and self-discipline stronger. Stories about situations that young children typically go through help them adjust to new experiences and learn coping skills.

Reading prepares children for school and college as well as the world of business. The library reading list for each grade level helps build a broader vocabulary and knowledge base. Using a dictionary to look up unfamiliar words expands and deepens your grasp of what is read.

CHAPTER FOURTEEN
SUCCESS

There are only two lasting bequests we can give our children ... one is roots, the other wings.

-- Stephen R. Covey, best-selling author

The man, Derrick, enjoys reading books to his son about successful people. He shares with him the formula for success. And he tells him often, "If you go by the formula and read the books of the rich and wise, you truly will be successful."

EMERY'S POINT

The art of Emery Franklin is narrative; meaning, it tells a story. The colors he applies have meaning too. In this painting called *Success*, he uses purple in the sky. The color purple stands for royalty, luxury, wealth, good judgment and spiritual fulfillment. There are also varied shades of green in the painting. The color green stands for life, nature and healing as well as money and love. Emery is a positive person who gives out positive vibes and creates positive art. He believes that negative art on your walls and negative videos can have a detrimental effect on your thinking.

The "Crossroads: From Sagging to Success" series of paintings starts with the end of slavery and finishes with success. This book demonstrates that, despite unfounded ideas of inferiority, there are plenty of successful people in our race – great inventors, poets, artists, writers, athletes, business people and outstanding African Americans in every walk of life. The more you read, the more you'll know them. Through reading and paying attention, you'll get to know billionaires like Oprah Winfrey, Robert Johnson, Michael Jordan and Earvin "Magic" Johnson. As you meet successful people, ask what books influenced them the most. No doubt they know the secret to success and practice the Law of Attraction daily.

The First Black President

On January 20, 2009, Barack Hussein Obama was inaugurated as the 44th president of the United States and the first African American president in American history.

Emery dreams of his painting of President Obama being part of the First Family's art collection and he is confident that God's Law of Attraction will make it happen. The painting is on loan to the Ninth District Congressman who has been asked to deliver it to the President. Emery smiles with delight, he knows Mr. Obama will enjoy the handsome portrait and he expects it to happen.

AFTERWORD

TAPPING INTO THE LAW OF ATTRACTION

Thank you for taking the time to read this book. Our purpose in writing has been to show how much African-American people have done to make the world a better place and to encourage you to think. Think more deeply than raiment and meat; life is more than what to wear or what to eat. Think more positively about yourself and the world around you. By reading this book, you also learned how the Law of Attraction works and how you can use it to make your dreams come true. If you can believe, you can achieve.

FROM FLORENCE

I have been writing books in my head since I was 12. Yet, this is the first book of mine that has ever been published, promoted and widely distributed. I thought I was an optimist until I met Emery and his wife Robbie. Emery had a different way of looking at things and at life. He put his hopes, dreams and desires out front – as if placing an order with the universe or God himself. And it works.

From Emery, I learned to take my God-given talent to its natural conclusion and not to wait for that talent to be recognized or harnessed by others. Once we worked together promoting his first public library exhibit, Emery simply stated that we should do a book together and I agreed. We didn't wait for someone to recognize our talent and ask us to do this book. That is part of the Secret: To know what you want and to ask for it, to believe that it will come to pass and then to start rejoicing as if you already have the thing or the experience that you desire.

I confess that I am a novice at the Law of Attraction which really has been in operation all of our lives. I am no stranger to its universal message. When our thoughts are positive, we do well. When they are negative, stuff happens and it seems that nothing goes right. The more we think on our problems, the more trouble comes. It goes just like that until we change our attitude and our thinking.

Make a decision that no matter what you have been told negatively about yourself, that you are so much more and that you have the power to be as great as you want to be. So, decide today to be great! Tap into your God-given genius.

As a man thinketh in his heart, so is he.
~ Proverbs 23:7

FROM EMERY

I have always wondered how people could live on the same street and one would be wealthy and one poor. Everyone has the same power. It is the way you think. If you think poor, if you dress poor, you become or stay poor.

Some times I stutter when I talk. My father, brother and sister all stuttered and grew out of it. When I was in the ninth grade, my mother said "Thank God that you can speak." That hit home and my stuttering never bothered me again. I talk to everybody. You can learn a lot from talking to people. You'll even see me talking on television. I still stutter and I'm glad I can talk.

Because I never let anything hold me back, I paint and play the piano too. I taught myself to play music. Anything I want to know, I can generally find in a book.

I went into real estate because I wanted to learn about property and property values. When I started reading the books that rich people read, I lived in a $55,000 house. My wife and I started visualizing ourselves in a better part of town. I landscaped my $50k house and put in a fish pond. I made the house look like a $70,000 house. My neighbors didn't like it. One said to me, "You act like you live in Germantown." I said, "I am."

Act like what you want to be.
I painted my house, added outdoor lights and installed a sprinkler system. On weekends, we went to look at brand-new houses – taking pictures, saying we would have to include this or that in our house and visualizing ourselves in that type of house.

Decide whatever you want to be.
I decided I wanted to earn my living as an artist. I paint 6 to 10 hours a day and sell my pictures online, on websites like www.emery-franklin.artistwebsites.com and in art galleries. I also have people who work with me to sell my artwork and I pay them a commission. Today, I live in a house that we had built on a lake. We picked out everything: The contractor had to give us what we wanted because we were the ones paying for it.

I get ideas for new paintings all the time. Right now, I have more than a dozen ideas for paintings in my head. For example, here is a painting of my friend Vernon Winfrey who lives in Nashville. Mr. Winfrey already owned two of my boxer pictures before I surprised him with this portrait. This is the first book that Florence and I have done, but it is not our last.

Portrait of Vernon Winfrey by Emery Franklin

Artist Emery Franklin and Vernon Winfrey, father of Oprah Winfrey

INVENTIONS AND INNOVATIONS
BY AFRICAN AMERICANS

If you knew how many everyday inventions and innovations have been worked on, created, modified, or improved Black Americans, you would never run out of material for book reports, experiments, special projects, or conversati Henry Baker in his book, *The Colored Inventor: A Record of Fifty Years*, published in 1913 recorded some 250 inventi patented by black people in the late 1800's and early 1900's.

Add to this list black inventors, like Madame C.J. Walker who invented black hair care products or Edmond Ber who invented the spark plug, that did not patent their inventions. Frederick McKinley Jones also never patented portable x-ray machine and it was later patented by someone else. A prolific inventor with 60 patents to his cre Jones invented because there was a need or a problem to be solved. Since 1821, when Thomas L. Jennings beca the first black person to receive a patent, there have been enumerable patents by creative and inventive black peo The majority of patents are for pre-existing items. For instance, did you know that Thomas Edison wasn't the person to invent a light bulb and that he invented more than 50 different ones.

SELECTED PATENTS BY BLACK INVENTORS

Invention	Patent No.	Date Patent Issued	Inventor	City of Record
Air conditioning/ Refrigeration unit** for long-haul trucks	2,475,841	July 12, 1949	Frederick M. Jones	Minneapolis, MN
Attachment for shuttle arm; device used to capture orbiting spacecraft	4,664,344	May 12, 1987	William D. Harwell	Houston, TX
Automatic Steam Engine Lubricator	129,843	July 23, 1872	Elijah McCoy	Ypsilanti, MI
Automated Elevator Doors	381,207	Oct. 11, 1887	Alexander Miles	Duluth, MN
Automatic Gear Shift	1,889,814	Dec. 6, 1932	Richard B. Spikes	San Francisco, CA
Automatic Shoe Lasting Machine**	274,207	Mar. 20, 1883	Jan E. Matzeliger	Lynn, MA
Bicycle Attachment	947,945	Feb. 1, 1914	George T. Sampson	New Haven, CT
Bicycle Frame*	634,823	1899	Isaac R. Johnson	Newport, RI
Broadband & wireless communication systems	7,120,139 (has 7 patents)	Oct. 10, 2006	Jesse Eugene Russell	Piscataway, NJ
Cash Register*	574,302/608,509	Dec. 29, 1896/Aug. 2, 1898	Lee S. Burridge	New York, NY
Casket-Lowering Device	529,311/664,581	Nov. 13, 1894 /Dec. 25, 1990	Albert C. Richardson	Frankfurt, MI
Combined knife & scoop			James A. Sweeting	New York, NY
Cooking Range*	180,323	July 25, 1876	Thomas A. Carrington	Baltimore, MD
Cotton Planter	15	Aug. 31, 1836	Henry Blair	Glen Ross, MD

Invention	Patent #	Date	Inventor	Location
Cotton Chopper*	520,888	June 5, 1894	George W. Murray	Rembert, SC
Cotton Seed Planter*	642,050	Jan. 13, 1900		Sumter, SC
Dry-Scouring (cleaning) *(first African American patent)*	3360x	Mar. 3, 1821	Thomas L. Jennings	New York, NY
Desktop Computer	4,528,626	July 9, 1985	Mark E. Dean	Boynton Beach, FL
Dust Pan*	587,607	Aug. 3, 1897	Lloyd P. Ray	Seattle, WA
Electric Railway Trolley*	505,370	Sept. 19, 1893	Elbert R. Robinson	Chicago, IL
Folding Bed*	629,286	July 18,1899	Leonard C. Bailey	Washington, DC
Food Preservative Chemicals	59 patents		Lloyd A. Hall	Born in Elgin, IL
Fountain Pen	419,065	Jan 7,1890	William B. Purvis	Philadelphia, PA
Gas Burner*	993,687	May 30, 1911	Benjamin F. Jackson	Jersey City, NJ
Gas Mask*	1,090,936	Mar. 24, 1914	Garrett A. Morgan	Cleveland, OH
Golf Tee*	638,920	Dec. 12, 1899	George F. Grant	Boston, MA
Heating Furnace**	1,325,905	Dec. 23, 1919	Alice H. Parker	Morristown, NJ
Helicopter*	3,065,933	Nov. 26, 1962	Paul E Williams	Washington, DC
Hot Comb*	1,362,823	Dec. 21, 1920	Walter H. Sammons	Philadelphia, PA
Ice Cream Scooper**	576,395	Feb 2,1897	Alfred L. Cralle	Pittsburg, PA
Induction Telegraph and 59 other patents	373,915	Nov. 29, 1887	Granville Woods	Cincinnati, OH
Ironing Board*	473,653	April 26, 1892	Sarah Boone	New Haven, CT
Lawn Mower*	624,749	May 9, 1899	John A. Burr	Agawam, MA
Lawn Sprinkler*	581,785	May 4, 1897	Joseph H. Smith	Washington, DC
Lemon Squeezer*	572,849	Dec. 8, 1896	John T. White	New York, NY
Letter Drop Mailbox*	462,096	Oct. 27, 1891	Philip B. Downing	Boston, MA
Street Railway Switch	430,118	June 17, 1890		
Currency Counting Tray	1,313,074	Aug. 12, 1919		
Light Bulb Filament*	252,386	Jan. 17, 1882	Lewis H. Latimer	New York, NY
Medicine Tray*	D283249	April 1, 1986	Joan Clark	Los Angeles, CA
Mop*	499,402	June 13, 1893	Thomas W. Stewart	Detroit, MI
Movie Ticket Dispensing Machine	2,163,754	June 27, 1939	Frederick M. Jones	Minneapolis, MN
Pencil Sharpener**	594,114	Nov. 23, 1897	John Lee Love	Fall River, MA
Portable Fire Escape*	440,322	Nov. 11, 1890	Daniel McCree	Chicago, IL
Postmarking and Canceling machine	585,075	June 22, 1897	William Barry	Syracuse, NY
Railway Air Brakes	137,350/795,243	Dec. 12, 1902 /July 18, 1905	Granville Woods	New York, NY
Refrigerator*	455,891	July 14,1891	John Stanard	Newark, NJ
Spring seat for chairs*	380,420	April 3, 1888	Albert B. Blackburn	Springfield, OH
Starter Generator**	2,475,842	July 12, 1949	Frederick M. Jones	Minneapolis, MN
Steam Table*	592,591	Oct. 26, 1897	George W. Kelley	Norfolk, VA
Street Sweeper*	558,719	Apr. 21, 1896	Charles B. Brooks	Newark, NJ
Surgical Needle*	2,389,355	Nov. 20, 1945	Dr. Charles Drew	Washington, DC
Toilet (Chamber Commode)	122,518	Jan. 9, 1897	Thomas Elkins	Albany, NY
Traffic Signal*	1,475,024	Nov. 20, 1923	Garrett A. Morgan	Cleveland, OH
Transmission and Gear Shifting Means*	1,936,996	Nov. 28, 1933	Richard B. Spikes	San Francisco, CA
Typewriter*	634,285/782,542	Oct. 3, 1899/Feb. 14, 1905	Lee S. Burridge	New York, NY
Vending Machine*	724,187	Mar. 31, 1903	James A. Joyce	Cleveland, OH
Window Cleaner*	483,359	Sept. 27, 1892	Anthony L. Lewis	Evanston, IL

Note: *new and useful improvement; ** improvement with major impact on society

EMERY'S READING LIST

Barna, George. *The Power of Vision: Discover and Apply God's Vision for Your Life & Ministry*. 3rd Edition. Ventura, Calif.: Regal, 2009.

Behrend, Genevieve. *Your Invisible Power and How to Use It*. Bottom of the Hill Publishing, 2010.

Dyer, Wayne W. *The Power of Intention: Learning to Create Your World Your Way*. Carlsbad, Calif.: Hay House, 2004.

Dyer, Wayne W. *Inspiration: Your Ultimate Calling*. Carlsbad, Calif.: Hay House, 2006.

Hawkins, David. *Power vs. Force: The Hidden Determinants of Human Behavior*. Carlsbad, Calif.: Hay House, 2002.

Hill, Napoleon. *The Law of Success in Sixteen Lessons*. Meriden, Conn.: The Ralston University Press, 1928.

Hill, Napoleon. *Think and Grow Rich* (Rev. ed.). New York: Fawcett Crest, 1960.

Kiyosaki, Robert T. *Rich Dad, Poor Dad: What the Rich Teach Their Kids about Money – That the Poor and Middle Class Do Not!*. Paradise Valley, Ariz.: TechPress, 1998.

Losier, Michael J. *The Law of Attraction: The Science of Attracting More of What You Want and Less of What You Don't*. New York, N.Y.: Wellness Central, 2006.

Peale, Norman Vincent. *The Power of Positive Thinking: A Practice Guide to Mastering the Problems of Everyday Living*.
New York: Simon & Schuster Audio, 2001.

The Secret (Extended Edition). Dir. Drew Heriot, et al. Perf. Rhonda Byrne, Bob Proctor, Rev. Dr. Michael Beckwith, Neale Donald Walsch, Jack Canfield. DVD. TS Production LLC, 2006.

Tolle, Eckhart. *A New Earth: Awakening to Your Life's Purpose*. New York: Penguin, 2005.

Wattles, Wallace D. *The Science of Success: The Secret to Getting What You Want*. New York: Fall River Press, 2007.

ABOUT THE AUTHOR

Florence M. Howard is a public relations specialist, facilitator, event coordinator, and journalist. During her career, she has written for newspaper, radio, television and the Internet and has managed numerous special events and grassroots campaigns, including Voter Empowerment, HIV/AIDS Awareness and Housing events. She has a special interest in economic and community development and works with community development organizations, colleges, nonprofits and governmental agencies to improve the quality of life in selected communities. In addition to owning her own business, she has served as executive director of the Jackson Madison County African American Chamber of Commerce in Jackson, Tennessee since 2009.

A Journalism graduate of the University of Memphis, she started her career in the production department of WREG-TV, News Channel 3, in Memphis then the flagship station of the New York Times Broadcasting Company. She later held positions as copywriter/coordinator of production services and assistant promotions manager. Promoted to director of community affairs for the station, she became executive producer of the *Knowledge Bowl*, a high school academic quiz program, and manager for their Emmy Award-winning *Kids Count* community affairs campaign that promoted the welfare of children and families through TV specials, vignettes and projects such as the Kids Count Forum (one special guest was Malcolm-Jamal Warner of *The Cosby Show*), Drop Everything and Read and the Coats For Kids for 12 years. In addition to establishing the quiz program and kids campaign, she also wrote the employee newsletter and directed the speakers' bureau that coordinated appearances for news personalities Pam Crittendon, Mary Beth Conley, Alex Coleman, Brian Teigland and others. She received a M.A. degree in Journalism from the University of Memphis in 1999 and subsequently has taught journalism/mass communications at the U of M and LeMoyne-Owen College. Active on community boards of directors, she is the 1998 winner of the Florence M. Howard Leadership Award from Big Brothers/Big Sisters of Greater Memphis and other awards.

She is president and founder of SSCOMM, Inc./Secret Shop Communicators, a public relations firm (www.sscommpr.com) in Memphis, Tenn. She is the mother of Derrick Keith, who was also a writer.

www.ingramcontent.com/pod-product-compliance
Lightning Source LLC
Chambersburg PA
CBHW042035150426
43201CB00002B/30